Praising and Worshipping Jesus from the Heart Through Psalms and Songs

MaryAnn Moses
PO Box 15063
Washington, DC 20003
moses.mary28@gmail.com

AuthorHouse™
1663 Liberty Drive
Bloomington, IN 47403
www.authorhouse.com
Phone: 1-800-839-8640

Published by AuthorHouse   02/21/2013

ISBN: 978-1-4817-1742-7 (sc)
ISBN: 978-1-4817-1740-3 (e)

Library of Congress Control Number: 2013903432

This book is printed on acid-free paper.

Scripture quotations marked (KJV) are taken from the King James Version Large Print Compact Bible copyright ©2005 Holman Bible Publishers. All rights reserved. The author notes that when referred to the Father, Son and Holy Spirit pronouns are capitalized. The author wishes not to acknowledge satan; therefore, his name is not capitalized.

Cover design by: Shalonda Moses
          bytheSpirit creative solutions

Acknowledgements

I would like to acknowledge Jesus as my Savior and Lord. He is the one who made this project possible. Before I was conceived in my mother's womb, God knew I was going to be a writer. He sat back, kept me covered and waited until I decided to put away foolish things and put my faith and trust totally in Him. I had to become obedient to His voice and His commands. God wants me to be a kingdom citizen. So I have to follow His plan for my life, follow His values and commandments, and remain rooted in His Word.

God bless all the Pastors, Teachers and Ministers that taught me the Word of God according to the scriptures in the Holy Bible. Thank You.

Thanks to my family for your encouragement and support.

Contents

Preface

This book was published not for a specific group of people, but for the individual to use in their personal praise and worship to God. This book is a book of psalms for thanksgiving and prayer and songs for praise and worship. These psalms/songs describe the relationship between an individual and God that acknowledges His glory and power. A psalm tells of God's good works; offers praise, expresses thanksgiving and shows adoration to God. Psalms can also be read as a prayer.

Psalm comes from a Greek word "psalmos" meaning "to pluck a string instrument." Psalms are written for the individual to read or sing. There is no specific music set to the inspirational lyrics in these psalms and songs because each individual praises the Lord differently. So sing and read each psalm or song to the Lord giving Him praise and worship from your heart.

i

I will praise thee, O LORD with my whole heart;
I will shew forth all thy marvelous works. I will be
glad and rejoice in thee: I will sing praise to thy
name, O thou most High. —*Psalm 9:1-2-KJV*

It is my prayer that when you read through this book, you
will give God the glory, gratitude and honor He
so deserves.

—*MaryAnn Moses*

My Testimony

One night or shall I say early one morning around 1:30am God woke me up and told me to write a song down. I said, "Write a song down, I can't even sing." God said, "I didn't ask you to sing, just write." "People are always praising me, but not enough worship. I want more worshippers. I also want true praise, praise from the heart where a testimony can be given." So I wrote the words that were given to me in my spirit. The name of the song is "Jesus is the Pathway."

God wants true praises. He wants us to praise Him from our heart because of who He is and what He has done for us. When I finished writing the song, I read over what I had written. Then I attempted to sing the words. I put the pad down and tried to go back to sleep. I tossed and turned for about ten minutes and then God said that He wasn't finished with me. He gave me another song to write; "Shelter Me." I looked at the words. I noticed the similarities in the two songs. God wanted me to know that I can trust Him totally and what His Word says will not come back void. He also wanted me to know that whatever decisions I made He is still with me; He will never leave me nor forsake me. Since that night He has given me psalms and several more songs to write. I am now more aware of how I treat people and live my life. I am not there yet, but I continue to strive to that place where God will say to me, "Well done, my good and faithful servant."

Why Praise and Worship God?

Praise ye the LORD. Praise God in his sanctuary: praise him in the firmament of his power.

Praise him for his mighty acts: praise him according to his excellent greatness.

Praise him with the timbrel and dance: praise him with stringed instruments and organs.

Praise him upon the loud cymbals: praise him upon the high sounding cymbals.

Let every thing that hath breath praise the LORD.

Praise ye the LORD. *—Psalm 150 (KJV)*

We are to praise and worship God because we are commanded in His Word to praise Him so we can have a proper relationship with Him. We praise God because He loves it (Psalm 22:3). We praise God because it brings victory, power and blessing in our life. We are to praise the Lord at all times (Psalm 34:1). Praise literally comes from the Hebrew word **"Judah"** meaning praise.

It also comes from the Hebrew words; **halal** meaning to extol, praise Him above other gods and **jah** meaning God or Lord. So when we say "**Hallelujah**" we are giving God the highest praise.

Praise means to extol, to magnify, to honor, and to show gratitude. Praise is given with admiration. Also the Hebrew word "**Todah**" means to extend hands; another form of praise.

Praise can be used as a spiritual weapon. The scriptures in the Holy Bible tell the importance of praise and why we should praise. Examples are found in: **I Chronicles 16:25-31, 2 Chronicles 20:21-22, Isaiah 42:8-10, John 4:23-24, Hebrews 13:15, Psalm 66:1-4 and 1 Peter 2:9.** The book of Psalm in the Holy Bible is full of praise and worship verses.

We praise God for who He is. He is our creator. We should worship Him and not His creations in the world. We thank Him for the creations. For if we worship the creations in the world, they become our gods. God is more than worthy to be praised. We praise God because He is the beginning (**Alpha**) and the end (**Omega**); the first and the last. He is in Genesis through Revelation. God is the King of Kings and the Lord of Lords. He is almighty. God dwells in the praises of His people. We praise God because of His power. He is excellent and great. God is holy and He has never ending mercy. Hallelujah!!! We are to praise God whether feeling good or bad. Praising God will lift your spirit. I know this for a fact. If I feel tired and don't feel like praising God at that moment I remember that we are to praise Him whether we feel like it or not. I then praise the Lord and end in worship. My body feels refreshed and my mind is renewed. We praise God in our trials. Praise is an action word. We praise God with our mouth, with joy, with gladness, with thankfulness, with songs, with psalms, with instruments, with laughter, with clapping and with dancing. We are to praise God with love. Love is an action word. If we say we love someone there should be some demonstration. Action speaks louder than words. God loves us so much. He showed how much He loves us by giving His only son, Jesus to die on the cross to pay the price for our sins.

Praise is a form of worship. Praise is to acknowledge what God has done and worship is to acknowledge who God is. The two go hand in hand. We worship God because He is worthy. Worship is intimate. Worship brings us close to the heart of God. We worship God for who He is, for what He has done, for what He is doing and for what He is going to do. Worship is a communion between God and man. Worship is giving to God. Worship is overpowering love for God. Worship is the out pouring of our inner being. We worship God with our mind, heart and body; by bowing down, kneeling or putting our face upward and extending hands as act of submission. In worship our focus should only be on God, honoring Him as our LORD. We must worship God in spirit and truth. To worship in truth we must have a pure heart, acknowledge our sin and repent, submit to His will and be obedient to His voice. True worship must come from the heart. **This is worth repeating.** True worship must come from the heart. I have seen people in worship services singing and supposedly worshipping, but looking all around at others, looking at their phones or talking. Their heart is not centered on God. I was guilty of this until I learned what true worship is. True worship will make our behavior more pleasing to God. He will reveal His presence to us during worship. It is a wonderful feeling to get in God's intimate presence, a feeling that cannot be expressed.

We must be sincere. God does not recognize **hypocritical worship**—worshipping Him and not changing our lifestyle or **worship rituals**—doing all the necessary things for worship (pray, give, praise), but not obeying God's commands and our life is full of sin.

We worship God by sharing and helping others, listening, doing good, tithing, praying, serving and sharing the good news of Jesus. We can worship God individually or corporately (in a group or church). We shall worship no other gods which includes, but not limited to cars, clothes, money, houses, shoes, or man.

> O praise the LORD, all ye nations: praise him,
> all ye people For his merciful kindness is great
> toward us: and the truth of the LORD endureth
> for ever. Praise ye the LORD. —*Psalm 117 (KJV)*

Psalms and Songs

1

A Worship Melody

God's grace and mercy—how sweet

I live because of you—

I was once blind, but now my eyes are open—to your will

I know of your goodness and I know that your word is true.

Thank you Jesus, thank you Jesus, thank you, thank you Jesus

I praise you Jesus, I praise you Jesus, praise you, praise you Jesus

I worship you Jesus, I worship you Jesus, worship, worship you, Jesus

Mighty is your name, mighty is your name, mighty is your name, Jesus

You are worthy, you are worthy, you are worthy Jesus

Hallelujah, hallelujah, hallelujah, hallelujah

I worship you, I worship you, worship you, Jesus

Hallelujah, hallelujah, hallelujah, hallelujah

A Worship Melody *(continued)*

I love you, I adore you, I bow down before you

You are wonderful, you are glorious, I worship you

Jesus, Jesus, Jesus, Jesus,

I worship you, worship you, worship you

Worship you, worship you, worship you

Jesus, Jesus, Jesus, Jesus

Worship, worship, worship, worship you Jesus

Angels

I have angels all around me, thank you Lord

Angels are in the front of me, angels are in the back of me, angels are to my left, angels are to my right

They protect me as I drive

They protect me as I shop

They protect me as I walk and they protect me as I talk

I have angels all around me, thank you Lord

Angels are in the front of me, angels are in the back of me, angels are to my left, angels are to my right

As I stand they are there beside me, as I sit they are right there with me to watch me, to help me and to protect me

I have angels all around me, thank you Lord

Call His Name

You call Him Wonderful

I call Him Master

You call Him Jehovah Jireh

I call Him my provider

You call Him Jehovah Shalom

I say He gives me peace

You call Him El Shadi

I say He is all that

I say Jesus, Jesus

He is the same—

Jesus, Jesus, Jesus

You say Emanuel

I say God is with me

You say trinity

I say He's three in one

Father, Holy Spirit, and Son

Call His Name *(continued)*

Jesus, Jesus, Jesus

Call His name

Chorus

Oh how I love to call His name

Wonderful, Master, Provider, Healer, My Peace

He's all that, He is the same—God is with me

Trinity, three in one—Father, Holy Spirit, and Son

Jesus, Jesus, Jesus

Oh how I love to call His name

Jesus, Jesus, Jesus, Jesus, Jesus, Jesus

I love calling His name

(Repeat Chorus)

Covered By the Blood

I'm covered by the blood— Covered by the blood of Jesus

I'm covered by the blood—Covered by the blood of Jesus

No weapon formed against me shall prosper because—

I'm covered by the blood of Jesus—Covered by the blood of the Lamb

He was nailed to the cross for me—He was nailed to the cross for me—He was nailed to the cross for me—That's why I'm covered by the blood of Jesus—Covered by the blood of the Lamb

He took the pain for me—He took the pain for me—He took the pain for me—That's why I'm covered by the blood of Jesus—Covered by the blood of the Lamb

I'm covered, Yes I'm covered, Covered by the blood of Jesus. I'm covered, Yes I'm covered, Covered by the blood of Jesus.

No weapon formed against me shall prosper—No…no… no weapon formed against me shall prosper because I'm covered by the blood of Jesus.

Covered By the Blood *(continued)*

He died and arose for me—He died and arose for me—He died and arose for me—

That's why I'm covered by the blood of Jesus—Covered by the blood of the Lamb

I'm covered by the blood—Covered by the blood of Jesus (Repeat 3 times)

No weapon formed against me shall prosper because

I'm covered by the blood of Jesus—Covered by the blood of the Lamb

Thank you Lord for your blood (Repeat 3 times)

Thank you Lord for covering me with your blood

A Conversation With God

My mother said I could always talk to you. So here I am. Do you hear me?

You said, "I always hear you my child"

I keep looking back over my past—

You said, "It is alright to glance back over your life to learn from your mistakes, and remember that it was I who pulled you through your storm, so keep moving forward"

I look down on myself—

You said, "Look up"

I want to drink—

I want to smoke—

I want to lie—

You said, "Don't try"

My days are sometimes dreary and dark—

You said, "It will get better, I am the light"

I feel like crying—

You said, "Cry", "In the morning will come joy"

A Conversation With God *(continued)*

I'm lonely—

You said, "You are never alone. I am always with you."

Who are you?—

You said, "King of Kings, Lord of Lords, the Creator of the universe,

Alpha and Omega—I am God Almighty

What's your name?—

You said, "My name is above all other names, I am called, "I Am", "El Shadai", "Jehovah Rophah", "Jehovah Shalom",

"Jehovah Jireh", "Yeshua"; it's alright to call me "Jesus", Jesus, Jesus

I will answer—just say Jesus, Jesus, Jesus

"I 'm always with you—You can call on Me night or day"

Jesus, Jesus, Jesus

You said, "Move forward, Look up, Don't try, it will get better—I promise"

A Conversation With God *(continued)*

And then you said

"Be patience, have faith, believe My word—I will comfort you and that you can depend on"

"I AM GOD"

And then I said,

Thank you God for talking with me.

He Is The King

Hallelujah—Hallelujah—Hallelujah—Jesus is the King (Repeat 2 times)

He's wonderful, He is awesome, He is mighty, He is the King (Repeat 2 times)

Hallelujah—Hallelujah—Hallelujah—Jesus is the King (Repeat 2 times)

He's magnificent, He's El Shaddi, He's all powerful—He is the King (Repeat 2 times)

Hallelujah—Hallelujah—Hallelujah—Jesus is the King (Repeat 2 times)

He is Jehovah, he is counselor, He is Yeshua—He is the King (Repeat 2 times)

Halle—lujah—halle—lujah—halle—lujah

(Back to the top)

Yes—Yes—Yes—Yes—

He is King, He is king, He is king

13

He's On My Side

He's on my side

When I think about the goodness of Jesus, I'm glad He's on my side

His goodness, grace and mercy endureth forever

When I think about the goodness of Jesus, I'm glad He's on my side

His goodness, grace and mercy endureth forever

He's on my side, He's on my side

Jesus shed His blood for me, He died for me

That's why I'm glad He's on my side

He's on my side, Yes He's on my side

He loves me unconditional, and I love Him too

He's on my side, Yes He's on my side

When I think of His goodness, grace and mercy, I'm glad He's on my side

Yes He's on my side

He's On My Side *(continued)*

He said that He will never leave me or forsake me

He's on my side, I'm glad He's on my side

Hold My Hand

Hold my hand—sweet Jesus, Hold my hand

Through the rain, through the storm, through the pain, hold my hand

Hold my hand—sweet Jesus, Hold my hand

Through the wilderness, hold my hand and pull me out

Through the hurt, through the brokenness, hold my hand

Hold my hand—sweet Jesus, Hold my hand

I don't want to fall, I don't want to stumble; I must move forward so—

Hold my hand sweet Jesus, hold my hand

I'll never, never let go—I'll never let go of your hand

The hands that were nailed to the cross where blood was shed for me—

Hold my hand sweet Jesus, hold my hand

I'll never let go—no, no, never let go of your hand so hold my hand

(Back to the top)

16

I'm Blessed

I'm blessed! I'm blessed! I'm blessed

I'm blessed by the Best, Jesus I'm blessed by the Best, Jesus

I'm blessed

I'm blessed in the country

I'm blessed in the city

I'm blessed at work

I'm blessed at church

I'm blessed! I'm blessed! I'm blessed!

I'm blessed by the Best, Jesus I'm blessed by the Best, Jesus

I'm blessed shopping

I'm blessed eating

I'm blessed living

I'm just blessed

I'm blessed by the Best, Jesus I'm blessed by the Best, Jesus

I'm just blessed!

(Repeat from the top)

I'm On My Way

I'm on my way to the Promised Land,

I'm on my way to the Promised Land,

I'm on my way to the Promised Land,

No turning back, no turning back

I'm on my way to Canaan Land,

I'm on my way to Canaan Land,

I'm on my way to Canaan Land,

I'm moving forward, I'm moving forward

I'm on my way where God is leading me,

I'm on my way where God is leading me,

I'm on my way where God is leading me,

I believe God, I believe His Word

I believe God, I believe His Word

So I'm on my way to the Promised Land

No turning back, I'm moving forward going where

God is leading me because I believe

Jesus Is Always There

When the devil tried to take me out…Jesus was there and pulled me in.

When I was blind and could not see…Jesus lead the way. He opened my eyes and now I see…Jesus was there for me.

Jesus turned my bitterness into sweetness, when I feel lonely He rocks me in His arms…Jesus is there.

He is with me always…through the storms He gives me cover, in my lonely nights He gives me comfort, through my battles He helps me to fight. He is always there.

I became wiser and stronger because Jesus was there. Open your heart and let Jesus in. He will be with you always. Trust and believe in Jesus, He is always there. He is always there. He is always there for you and for me.

Chorus

Jesus you are there, yes you are there for me—He's with me and He's with you too—Just open up your heart and let Him in—He'll be with you through the storms, through your trials, through your sickness, through your battles, through your loneliness

Jesus Is Always There *(continued)*

Trust and believe in Jesus—He's always there—always there for you and for me.

(Return to top)

Repeat chorus two times.

Jesus You Are My Shelter

Jesus you are my shelter. Thanks for your covering. You have sheltered me in times of trouble and during my many storms.

Thank you Jesus for providing for me.

I praise you Jesus for making a way for me

You gave me refuge, you were my sanctuary

Jesus You promised that You will never leave me or forsake me

And I know this to be true because you see

When I had nowhere to go you were there in a hurry; You covered me, You gave me shelter

Thanks for Your shelter

When I could not see where I was going; You lighted my path

When I would worry, You said don't worry have faith

I was dwelling on the past and Jesus You brought me to the present

Jesus You Are My Shelter *(continued)*

You never gave up on me—Hallelujah

Jesus thanks for Your shelter

I praise you Jesus and I will dwell in your secret place and trust in You always because you are my God—Hallelujah! Hallelujah! Hallelujah! Amen

Just Want To Thank You

I just want to thank you, thank you, thank you

Just want to thank you for this day

Thank you, thank you Jesus

Hallelujah!! Thank you for another day

I just want to thank you for this day

Thank you for my strength

Thank you for my health

Thank you for my finances

I just want to thank you, thank you, thank you

Just want to thank you for this day

Thank you, thank you for another day

Hallelujah!! Thank you for another day

I just want to thank you for this day

You woke me up this morning

Thank you for grace and mercy this day

I give you praise, honor and glory

Just Want To Thank You *(continued)*

Hallelujah!! Thank you for another day

I just want to thank you for this day

You woke me up this morning

I give you praise, honor and glory

Just want to thank you

Thank you, thank you Jesus

Thank you, thank you Jesus

Thank you, thank you Jesus

Just want to thank you for this day

Just want to thank you for this day

Hallelujah, hallelujah, hallelujah

Lord I Love You

LORD—I love you

LORD—I love you

LORD— I need you to guide my life

LORD—I love you

LORD—I love you

LORD—I need you so I can be an example to the people I meet far and near

LORD—I love you

LORD—I love you

LORD—I need you to do your will and to walk like you walked when you were here

LORD—I love you

LORD—I love you

LORD—I love you

Lord I love you

To guide my life

Lord I Love You *(continued)*

So I can be an example

To do your will

To walk like you

I LOVE YOUUUUUUUUU

LORD—I need you

LORD—I need you

To guide my life

So I can be an example

To do your will

To walk like you

LORD I JUST NEED YOU!!!!!!

Loving You Lord

I love you Lord, I love you Lord today, tomorrow and forever

I love you Lord, I love you Lord today, tomorrow and forever because I have life eternal now

I love you Lord, I love you Lord today, tomorrow and forever because I have life eternal now

I love you. You are my strength, you are my hope,you are my everything

I love you. You are my strength, you are my hope, you are my everything

I love you Lord, I love you Lord today, tomorrow and forever

I love you, I praise you, I worship you for you are my Lord, my Father, my King and I will sing I love you, I love you Lord today, tomorrow and forever (Repeat two times)

Praise and Worship

I will lift my hands to praise—Praise Him, Praise Him, Praise Him

Father, Son and Holy Ghost

I will use my mouth to shout Hallelujah—Hallelujah, Hallelujah, Hallelujah to His name—Jesus, Jesus, Jesus

I will dance before my King—to praise Him—Praise Him, Praise Him, Praise Him

Father, Son and Holy Ghost

I will bow down to worship Him—Worship Him, Worship Him, Worship Him

Jesus, Jesus, Jesus

Lift my hands to Praise; Use my mouth to shout Hallelujah, Dance before my King, and Bow down to Worship God

Lift my hands to Praise; Use my mouth to shout Hallelujah, Dance before my King, and Bow down to Worship God

Praise and Worship *(continued)*

Praise Him, Praise Him, Praise Him

Bow before Him and worship Him, Bow before Him and worship Him, Bow before Him and worship Him

Worship Him, Worship Him, Worship Him, Worship, Worship, Worship, Worship Him

Shelter Me

Jesus shelters me—

In times of storms—When the winds blow

(Solo)

He shelters me—

During my trials—When problems arise—

Jesus is always there to shelter me—just believe

No more worrying—No more wondering how or why—

Just believe in your heart that He is there

Jesus will shelter you, and I know He shelters me—

(Chorus)

Oh, let the storms come—

Let the winds blow—

I know He shelters me 'because I believe

(Solo)

Shelter Me—

Shelter Me—

Shelter Me *(continued)*

Lord, I believe

No more worrying—No more wondering how or why—

Just believe in your heart that He is there

Jesus will shelter you, He shelters me

(Chorus)

Oh, let the storms come—

Let the winds blow—

I know He shelters me 'because I believe

Oh yes I believe

(All)

Shelter me, Shelter me—Lord, I believe—

I won't have to worry; I won't have to wonder how or why

Because I know He will be there to shelter me

Thank you Lord for sheltering me

Take My Hand

Take my hand Holy Spirit

Guide me through this weary land

Take my hand Holy Spirit

Lead me on………………..

Take my hand Holy Spirit

Let me walk with thee….

Take my hand Holy Spirit

Let me follow your ways…….
Take my hand Holy Spirit

Lead me on………………

(Repeat 2 times)

Thanks for the Cross

Thank God for the cross

I thank God for the cross

I thank God for the cross on Calvary

Thank God for the cross

I thank God for the cross

I thank God for the cross on Calvary

He shed His blood for me, He shed His blood for me, Jesus shed His blood for me on the cross

Thank God for the cross, thank God for the cross, I thank God for the cross on Calvary

He died on the cross, He died on the cross, Jesus died on the cross for me

Thank God for the cross, thank God for the cross, I thank God for the cross on Calvary

He arose three days later, He arose three days later, Jesus arose three days later from the tomb

Thank God for the cross, thank God for the cross, I thank God for the cross on Calvary

Thanks For The Cross *(continued)*

Thanks for the cross

He's alive in my heart, He's alive in my heart, Jesus is alive in my heart today

He's alive in my heart, He's alive in my heart, Jesus is alive in my heart today

Thank God for the cross, thank God for the cross, I thank God for the cross on Calvary

Thank God for the cross, thank God for cross, I thank God for the cross on Calvary

Hallelujah, Hallelujah, Hallelujah, Amen

Through the Open Door

You must be humble; you must pass the test to go through the open door

Money will cometh, Healing will cometh, Wisdom will cometh

Get up and walk through the open door

Get up and walk through the open door Get up and walk through the open door

Pray, pray, and pray Walk through the open door

Do what God says Walk through the open door

Follow God's plan for your life Walk through the open door

No more fear, no more pain, no more debt

Get up and walk through the open door

No more fear, no more pain, no more debt

Get up and walk through the open door

Money will cometh, Healing will cometh, Wisdom will cometh

Through The Open Door *(continued)*

Just get up and walk, just get up and walk, just get up and walk—

Through the open door

You must be humble; you must pass the test to go through the open door

Money will cometh, Healing will cometh, Wisdom will cometh

Get up and walk, Get up and walk, Get up and walk through the open door

Welcome

Welcome into my heart, Welcome into my heart

Lead me –Guide me, Show me the way

Welcome into my heart, Welcome into my heart

Lead me—Guide me, Show me the way

Welcome into my life, Welcome into my life

I love you—I need you, Stay with me

Welcome into my life, Welcome into my life

I love you—I need you, Stay with me

Oh Holy One, Jesus, Oh Holy One, Jesus, Oh Holy One, Jesus

Welcome into my heart, Welcome into my heart

Welcome into my heart, Welcome into my heart

(Repeat from the top)

Accepting Jesus as Your Lord and Savior

Have you ever thought where you would go when you die? Heaven or hell? Heaven being a glorious place where you can live for eternity; and hell a place of fire and tormenting heat where there is burning of the flesh, hollering and screaming daily.

I am sure you would choose Heaven; a place of peace, no sickness, no bills, no worries. You can be assured of living in this place for eternity right now. Just clear your mind and make a decision to accept Jesus into your heart. How can I do this? I am glad you asked. Open your mouth and say these words, believe what you are saying and mean it from your heart (Romans 10:9). Jesus is a just God. He will forgive and forget your sins and all wrong doings from your past (1John 1:9).

Lord Jesus I repent of all my sins and wrong doings, please forgive me.

I believe that you died on the cross and shed your blood for me.

I also believe that you arose from the grave three days later.

Come into my heart Jesus. I accept you as my Lord and Savior.

I want you to be a part of my life daily, lead me and guide me daily.

I am covered by your blood. I thank you for your blood. I thank you for your forgiveness.

In Jesus name, Amen

You are now saved. Welcome to the family of God!!

Romans 10:13

Now that you have taken the step of faith, find a church to attend where the pastor preaches and teaches according to the word and scriptures in the Holy Bible. Begin reading and studying the bible for yourself.

satan is mad at you now for giving your life to Jesus, but the angels are rejoicing. Continue to pray, praise and worship God daily, read the bible and stay around positive people.

Personal Testimony

Personal Testimony

_____

_____

_____

_____

_____

_____

_____

_____

_____

_____

_____

_____

_____

_____

_____

_____

_____

_____

_____

_____

_____

_____

_____

_____

Personal Testimony

Personal Testimony

_____

_____

_____

_____

_____

_____

_____

_____

_____

_____

_____

_____

_____

_____

_____

_____

_____

_____

_____

_____

_____

_____

_____

_____

I will extol thee, my God, O king; and I will bless thy name for ever and ever. Every day will I bless thee; and I will praise thy name for ever and ever. Great is the LORD, and greatly to be praised; and his greatness is unsearchable.

One generation shall praise thy works to another, and shall declare thy mighty acts. —*Psalm 145:1- 4*

Amen